Copyright © 2022 Tekkan
Artwork Copyright © 2022

All rights reserved.
First Printing, 2022
ISBN 978-1-0880-2525-3

To contact Tekkan please email:
buddhaboy1289@gmail.com

Table of Contents

Thic Nhat Hanh. . . . . Page 38

Thirty-eight Years Ago . . . . . . .Page 51

Edward Scissorhands . . . . Page 78

How to Read My Poems

I want to be direct in my meaning — I want people to clearly understand my meaning. My wordiness is inspired by Shakespeare, and the (aimed-for) concision is in imitation of Japanese style. Using the sonnet with the tanka, I mix the sensibility of the Occident and the Orient — which I have done by living in England, Japan, and America.

I have married the sonnet to the tanka. I tell a story in the sonnet. The story builds to a conclusion in the last line. The tanka is a commentary, or a counterpoint, to the sonnet — the combined poems have two endings.

Recently I have added haiku, limericks, and doggerel into my repertoire. The limericks have a rhyme scheme but the tanka do not.

I don't punctuate much in my poetry. I want the words themselves to do the work. There is logic between words, and the forms provide structure. By not using punctuation I hope to direct readers to carefully attend to each word — to appreciate the graininess of words.

Reading my poems silently and reading them aloud may be different experiences. There's not always a pause intended at the end of the line.

Hint: *sonnets are to be recited not as lines but as phrases, and a phrase sometimes overflows the break at the end of a line. I pause and take a breath where it seems natural for me to pause. Another person may pause differently than I do.*

Each poem is a piece of a mosaic, and it is my hope that the collection of poems forms a portrait of consciousness.

My friend, *Will Ersland*, is a wonderful artist. His artwork graces this book.

I am Barry MacDonald. I received the *dharma* name *Tekkan*, which means "Iron Man," a settled practitioner of great determination.

— *Tekkan*

Everyday Mind XXVI

Cottonwood branches
in fresh brilliant light —
cold burns my skin.

In January in Minnesota
The landscape is buried in heaps of snow
The dark and cold are a dreary combo
Any skin exposed to the wind feels raw
We patiently wait for happenstance thaws
The passage of time is terribly slow
So I look to upturn the status quo
And provide myself a touch of hoopla
By picturing exotic flamingos
They are visions of loveliness in pink
Their curving necks appear like question marks
They help me to forget my frozen toes
Flamingos live in paradise I think
The contrast with Minnesota is stark.

It doesn't quite work
to escape Minnesota
by seeing happenstance
plastic flamingos encased
in a landscape of piled snow.

My reliable buddy is Kitcat
He reminds me of a mountain lion
No — he doesn't share the same kind of brawn —
He pounces and wrestles with the doormat
I feed him so well he's a little fat
He stretches in the sun and also yawns
Mostly it's houseflies that he preys upon
He springs and lunges like an acrobat
And Kitcat possesses a cougar's eyes
That appear quite dangerous when he stares
He saunters about with aggressive grace
Like a predator — but only pint-sized —
The house is encumbered with tawny hair
I like to seize his head and stretch his face.

I don't suppose a
mountain lion would allow me
to pin back his ears
and stretch out his entire
face — but Kitcat doesn't mind.

I rest the palm of a hand on his head
And pull both of his ears backward gently
Which is just my way of being friendly
And I see that his mouth begins to spread
Into a wide smile which could be misread
As goofy — his eyes are bulging widely
As I stretch — I'm tugging only slightly —
Kitcat is composed as he looks ahead
And from his calm demeanor I can tell
That he is happy lying next to me
On the couch — I stop pulling his face and
Push his ears down instead as we both dwell
In my living room watching the T.V. —
I pat the top of his head with my hand.

I can't imagine
other animals or
people letting me
play with their faces and ears
except for happy Kitcat.

The oak the ash and the maple on the
Shelf of a limestone bluff that looks over
The river valley are sights that confer
Quiet familiarity on a
Cold morning as we gather around a
Fire inside a portable container
And we do enjoy gazing at the fire
And we take such pleasure in watching the
Horizon brighten as the sun is rising
Up but hasn't yet crested — as we meet
Again for our talk — which may be crazy —
But we gather such strength by exchanging
Simple and honest words that help defeat
Fear and isolation — we aren't lazy.

After a person
has been sober for a while
alcoholism
becomes an afterthought — we
come for the conversation.

The flamingos aren't separate from the
Tropics the water and the algae that
They feed on and if they didn't eat that
Type of algae then they wouldn't be the
Curiosity that they are and the
Epitome of exotica that
I love to think about while knowing that
They are that pigment pink because of the
Algae they consume just as their very
Odd yet graceful necks and their spindly stick
Legs are at one with the temperate air
And with the shallows of the lakes and seas
Where they live — and it really is a trick
Of nature to appreciate and share.

North America
creates bald eagles finches
crows pileated
woodpeckers in addition
to pink plastic flamingos.

A box in my living room stopped working
A week ago so I wasn't able
To fixate on my favorite cable
T.V. shows and I know when I'm watching
That I am wasting my time absorbing
Toxic news that is unbelievable
With murders that are inconceivable
And so for a week I was relaxing
And dwelling within the quiet of my
Home lounging about with serenity
Separated from the cultural trash
Liberated from political lies
Free of the scripted personalities
Living without American mishmash.

A techie replaced
the broken cable box — and
television is
not as bad as alcohol
or cigarettes I suppose.

I look at the way that Kitcat saunters
In the living room when he pounces on
A pitiful mouse when he sets upon
A fly in the air and when he wanders
Through the house I think he is a wonder
Of physicality of predation
As he attacks without hesitation
And he is such a natural fighter
Then I think about a mountain lion
Wandering the highlands in winter
Hunting deer rabbit elk sheep or raccoon
As it saunters and alerts and lies in
Wait before it pounces — mad with hunger —
Wayfaring under the light of the moon.

He is not hungry and
is under no compulsion
to wander and hunt
and yet Kitcat is alive
at night — and rushes about.

Greetings to the sun — the maker of days
No stigma of waywardness touches you
Your fire is good mighty and ever new
You hold the life of each season in sway
Not for an instant is the earth astray
You are a sparkle in a drop of dew
You are reflective off the oceans too
You are the pivot of our life today
We owe our beating hearts and breath to you
You are what makes the colors visible
Yours is the light that illumines the moon
Every single tree reaches up to you
Your radiation is reliable
We mark a daily pinnacle at noon.

You are a balance of
crushing gravity and
gaseous combustion
that does inspire
imagination.

However fierce a mountain lion is
It doesn't carry anger in its heart
Surely it can rip a body apart
Watching stalking and waiting when it does
Tearing ripping and biting as it does
It's doing no more than playing its part
Performing a role that nature imparts
But it doesn't suffer self-hypnosis
We are people who aren't hunting our prey
We visit delis and supermarkets
We are organized efficient killers
Some of us aspire to be gourmets
As predators we are the exorbitant
But see how many suffer from anger.

An angry heart can
claw and rip and tear and bite
a human body
apart — all needlessly so —
from delusional motives.

Humans are prone to intoxication
Dominance is a brutal elixir
We say we want to make the world better
We have experts who provide prescriptions
Bureaucracies dispense instructions
Politicians lionize go-getters
Our systems are always getting smarter
We pride ourselves on robust production
But with persistance and careful awareness
It becomes obvious over time that
So much of what our leaders do turns out
To be deceitful and quite egregious
And then we can see it's apparent that
Society promotes dishonest louts.

Cynicism's not
healthy and compassion and
self-forgetting love
are real human virtues —
but don't trust politicians.

The idea of the sun is tricky
Without eyes I wouldn't recognize it
And without skin I couldn't caress it
I am grateful to be able to see
To appreciate what it means to be
It is easy to be a hypocrite
To believe in things that are counterfeit
Even my own opinions disagree
I do misunderstand reality
I give them no thought — yet my heart pulsates
And my chest swells and it empties of breath
There's grace and rhythm in simplicity
And endless confusion inside debates
Is consciousness really curtailed by death?

The sun exists in
the sparking of synapses
and in optic nerves
and the sun also orbits
inside of the Milky Way.

Outside the window and down a small hill
There's a white wooden fence that I can see
At one of its corners there is a tree
The fence doesn't move — it only stands still
Watching everyday there aren't many thrills
But every yard contains a panoply
Which is a sampling of reality
It is another quiet day until
A squirrel is scampering atop the fence
The fence is curving and goes up and down
The squirrel goes up and down and along
This is an ordinary happenstance
The squirrel likes the fence to get around
I think this sight is worth a little song.

When it gets to the
corner the squirrel jumps and
precariously
seizes ahold of a twig
and pulls itself to safety.

George Oppen is a poet I admire
He wrote a book — *On Being Numerous*
I think his book is sadly humorous
It's about the isolation we share
Of the desperation behind our stares
And of the cruelty that shatters us
Harrowing nightmares that we don't discuss
Of nagging thoughts that our lives are haywire —
There is a brick that the eye picks in a
Wall of bricks so quiet of a Sunday
That was waiting for you here Mary-Anne
He writes thinking of clarity in a
Sense of transparency — he doesn't say
What it means — he doesn't say that he can.

There is clarity
And transparency
silent clarity
but George doesn't mean
much can be explained.

If you'd like to escape the madness of
Our time you should read the *Ramayana*
A creation myth of the Brahmana
There are many ideals it speaks of
Such as ethics and loyalty and love
It's the heroic journey of Rama
Who kills the king of demons — Ravana —
Valmiki wrote characters whom I love
Such as Hanuman who is a monkey
He's the son of Vishnu the god of wind
He's a spy who leaps over an ocean
Hanuman is honored for loyalty
He's impetuous generous and kind
An avatar of divine emotion.

Ravana has ten
heads and twenty arms — he steals
Rama's wife Sita
and Rama leads an army
of bears apes and monkeys.

Thomas is a little blue tank engine
Percy's even smaller and he is green
And they are buddies on the railroad team
Then Bill and Ben are mischievous twins
James is brilliant scarlet and he is vain
Diesel is nasty holds grudges and schemes
Gordon's dynamic and really blows steam
When Thomas fouls up he feels such chagrin
These are the engines on "Thomas and Friends"
A children's show of a T.V. series
That my kids watched growing up in Japan
A childhood fantasy of odds and ends
Mornings were noisy with cheerful stories
Thomas is boisterous and I'm a fan.

Inside a small room
in the middle of a
little drab rowhouse
was a scene of tooting
and puffing tomfoolery.

I drove a scooter searching in Kyoto
I wore a poncho in summer showers
And a thick leather jacket in winter
There were many days when I would just go
I was a youthful roving dynamo
I visited each of Kyoto's toy stores
Hungrily seeking Thomas characters
I wanted them all and couldn't let go
Trevor the tractor was hardest to find
I hunted for him for two dreary years
I tramped department stores in rubber boots
The elusive tractor disturbed my mind
I was an adult — I didn't shed tears —
There did come a day when I found my loot.

Thirty years later
all the Thomas characters
are in a box in
my basement forgotten by
Joshua and Jocelyn.

I loved a dancer when I was twenty
I wrote a sonnet that I was proud of
About a candle innocence and love
When dancing nude she fascinated me
Ragged desire wouldn't let me be
Who cares that most people would disapprove?
Young and rootless — I had nothing to lose
I was empty innocent and naïve
I wrote lines while riding city buses
It's a pity that I couldn't know her
It was imagination that I loved
Daydreaming of kisses and caresses
She lives in me — a make-believe lover —
I do remember her when I am bored.

I translated her
womanly beauty into
adoring words that
embody a longing that's
still fresh through many decades.

I live in a house on a quiet street
It's a pleasure to hear the wind and chimes
I'd say their notes do variously rhyme
In boisterous blusters they sound offbeat
However they jangle they are upbeat
Perhaps the wind is a musical mime
The play of the notes is a pantomime
The daily performance is very sweet
I do often wonder what makes the sound
Is it the chimes or the breezes that sing?
On occasion the chimes will clang in wind
The wind strikes the tubes and vibrates around
I think that the vibrating air has wings
The song of chimes arises in my mind.

Without vibrating
air there isn't stimulus
without listening
ears and an open mind there
isn't reverberation.

Everything around us comes from the earth
Earth is below and also above us
Earth is about and even inside us
The wind the seas the sky come from the earth
The water in our cells comes from the earth
Its teeming biology nurtures us
Its mineral chemistry supports us
Bodily elements come from the earth
We can feel the earth is truly alive
We are its breathing manifestations
Do we understand it sufficiently?
Without its workings we couldn't survive
We are infused with its fluctuations
May we feel it and tread differently.

We and the earth are
not separate entities
we didn't come from
elsewhere — we aren't others —
but we are one and the same.

I'm not doing what I'm supposed to do
That is what the critic inside me thinks
A punishing impulse that becomes a jinx
There's the daily news to drag myself through
Crafting opinions is what I should do
Smartly addressing society's kinks
Absorbing data establishing links
Confabulating solutions on cue
There are factions of ideology
Systems of thought dividing our people
Strong emotions that are based on belief
Inspiring endless pathology
Creating a cancer — eating people —
What can be written to foster relief?

To argue over
the lies and oppressions of
the use of power
is an endless ambition
summoning pitiless words.

I think there is always liberation
To be found in relaxation and if
I can manage to relax even if
I'm having discouraging emotion
And feeling an impulse of aggression
I could lift the weight from my shoulders if
I pay attention to my breathing if
I let go of endless complication
As I always have the luxury and
Leisure of drawing oxygen into
My lungs and I can close my eyes also
And with every breath there is peace at hand
There is nothing more that I have to do
I can surrender thought — and just be slow.

Outside the window
on the hedge chickadees
hop turn and flit off.

It's not so easy to imagine it
What would the earth be like without people?
In our absence would the planet be dull?
The life of the species would be well-knit
Cattle and chickens could relax a bit
The shores of oceans would host the seagulls
Their plaintive calls would remain an earful
But there wouldn't be humans to hear it
We impose self-consciousness on the earth
We dominate and rearrange nature
We argue and fight and make decisions
It is to the earth that we owe our birth
Insanity is part of our nature
Compounded with intelligent vision.

The cosmos birthed
restless and dissatisfied
self-consciousness and
even distant galaxies
may be encompassed.

Does the universe use my eyes to see?
I loiter at my desk and play with words
I gaze outside and encircle the birds
Does cosmic consciousness encompass me?
What is the impact of society?
Mass emotions are so often absurd
The result of adversity is blurred
What is the meaning of being empty?
I take such comfort in a vast blue sky
The moon's a homely companion at night
Thought of light years is disorienting
What good does it do to tell myself lies?
Bantering stories is my heart's delight
Breathing wholeheartedly is relaxing.

I am not and could
never be isolated
and alone within
these interpenetrating
haunting beautiful questions.

My poetry is a sunrise diary
I look for treasure in each of my days
Whatever life presents is A-OK
There are times of creeping anxiety
When I seek for balancing clarity
It's healthy to juggle with words and play
Pretending to host an *auto-da-fé*
There's irony in mock calamity
Every day has its own peculiar touch
I'd like to capture transience on paper
I want to communicate life to you
It's better not to expect very much
This is only glorified notepaper
A rhyming propitious whoop-de-do.

I scribble every
morning as the sun rises
and a bald eagle
just adjusted its wings in
a turn over the maple.

Hints of the poem are in the first line
Fresh is the snowfall that came overnight
Bright is the sunshine that helps me to write
Blind is the heart that is adamantine
I play with words and nonsensical rhymes
The pith of thought is depressingly trite
The weight of these words is gossamer light
I sit in a chair and while away time
Confabulate rhythm — forget the sense
Accumulate questions — abandon force
Approximate wisdom — don't try too hard
This poem is worth a couple of cents
These lines are obvious and are not coarse
My poem is lazy but it's not a canard.

I'm only playing
games today and I'm hoping
you're not serious —
the hair of my mustache
and on my chin became white.

She is a woman who stimulates seeds
She's a ragamuffin angelic girl
She has a head of thick natural curls
It's hard to know where attraction will lead
Longing is wretched and has made me bleed
I see my thoughts are beginning to swirl
I want to avoid a compulsive whorl
How can I separate my wants and needs?
I know for certain I can't control her
When together our talking is easy
I'd like to be tender — not push too much
The minute I do is when I'll lose her
The tug of desire makes me gutsy
She knows especially I want to touch.

She gave me two
of her knit hats
suffused with her
perfume — she knows
what she's doing.

There is no simpler method than doing
My wholehearted best while letting go of
Results especially with those whom I love
Because controlling them isn't loving
Imposing my will is self-defeating
Which I know from experience would shove
Them away from me when I want to move
Closer — simplicity is exhausting —
I want them to do what they want to do
They have perfect freedom to live their lives
Even if they choose to be without me
So the question becomes what do I do
When my thoughts are filled with self-doubting lies
When I am feeling ragged and empty?

I don't think I'm meant
to be comfortable and
indolent all the
time but I do need to learn
the art of relaxation.

Figuring out what I'm supposed to be
Doing is a question of making moves
And seeing what happens and I do shove
When I believe that it's necessary
To clarify an ambiguity
And I don't know what it is that I love
Unless I'm wholeheartedly a part of
The game of life with curiosity
Pushing up against my limitations
And seeing which it is that makes me — me —
Against difficulty disappointments
Being flexible with fluctuations
Seeking an intelligent repartee —
Because life questions and doesn't relent.

Am I doing life
or is life doing me?
There is provoking
repartee with love
and resonance.

I adore my chair and keyboard and the
Window that I look through in the morning
When I get to my desk — I love playing
With words and having them skip along a
Page easily and as lazy as a
Happy child — I like letting out a string
Of thought — I enjoy the job of coiling
The ends of lines with rhymes that may be a
Trick that a reader doesn't take the time
To notice — I look forward to the end
Of this poem — now I don't have a clue —
The momentum is building line to line —
I do hope this poem doesn't offend
My only goal is to entertain you.

What did you want?
Did you want something
Serious?

It's a pain that America depends
Upon the media's information
That's saturated with accusation
That makes it so difficult to defend
Disfavored views even among my friends
Mass opinion imposes force upon
Outsiders exerting the dominion
Of the nation's cleverest who pretend
To be civic-minded while instead it's
True they've mastered the art of accusing
Opponents of the very evils that
They themselves are guilty of and so it's
Good to be poised and not be the playthings
Of the propaganda of the autocrats.

Will we be ruled by
the cleverest and the most
ruthless among us
as propaganda is a
timeless tool of tyranny?

Accusation is a clever trick of
Misdirection as public attention
Focuses on the accused and not on
The accuser who is safely above
Suspicion because of the gimmick of
Hatred aroused by the circulation
Of slyly distorted information —
We need the strength of deeply rooted love
Of sincerity and integrity
That are precious qualities of the heart
Of courageous cultural warriors
Opposed to lies who then become lonely
Figures misunderstood and set apart
And targeted within the info-war.

For the innocent
and naïve the secrets and
inner workings of
society are almost
incomprehensible.

I do take a partisan point of view
I compose scorching editorials
Opposing hypocritical cabals
And over decades I've gotten used to
The taste of bitterness I attend to
But in my poems I don't want to brawl
I won't touch upon the issues at all
Because arguments divide me from you
Details of issues disappear with time
People are prone to bickering and war
I do a little to promote justice
It's a lot more fun to compose my rhymes
Partisan politics is just a bore
Poetry is my relaxing device.

Because I edit
an obscure little journal
of opinion I'm
not widely known or well paid
but I avoid the death threats.

It's a shame that more people cannot see
How America could be on the verge
Of losing so much as there is a surge
Of hatred that's dividing our country
With factions not bothering with mercy
With disapproved opinions being purged
And the death of free speech deserves a dirge
It's a pity to think how could it be
So many of our children are murdered
Not intentionally — by accident —
These kids are caught in the crossfire and shot
For media these deaths aren't worth a word
The gang violence is inconvenient
With expendable deaths — that's the upshot.

Kids who aren't being
justly educated and
are abandoned by
society don't add up
to political leverage.

Politics resembles psychodrama
And its personalities are brittle
The usual game is to belittle
Opponents with fabricated trauma
Concocted slanders depending on the
Lunatic factions sprinkling a spittle
I do my best to be noncommittal
Indifferent to the melodrama
But then the spectacle is sobering
Because politicians are serious
Apparently immune to feeling shame
While their narratives are mesmerizing
And their agendas are imperious
They are experts at utilizing blame.

Righteousness
turns opponents
into demons.

I do believe that there are honest men
And women of both parties who do their
Best to make decisions based on a fair
Reading of issues and we do depend
Upon courtesy and grace to befriend
All sorts of people who sincerely care
About decency and with whom we share
Our nation and with whom we may contend
And argue over the economy
On the difficult issues of justice
Working toward a peaceful coexistence
Supporting widely spread prosperity —
Revolutionaries are among us
American liberty needs defense.

Marxist ideology
pits classes and races
against each other
using hostility
to seize power.

Sincerity and integrity are
Ideals and liberty is a worthy
Cause and editorials are weighty
With thoughtful aggression designed to spar
And I've fabricated a repertoire
Of favorite views to push cleverly
But arguing doesn't make me happy
Accumulated bitterness leaves scars
It's true that warriors serve a purpose
They sacrifice their lives for a mission
Taking comfort in sister/brotherhood
We have a cherished legacy to lose
There is *esprit-de-corps* to draw upon
And yet I could forget it all for good.

Do opposing
warriors mirror
each other in
sincerity and
integrity?

Thic Nhat Hanh

A peace activist poet and teacher
A lovely Buddhist Vietnamese monk
Has died in Plum Village taking a chunk
From my heart to lose such a world leader
Such an open-hearted peaceful seeker
Of harmony who through his life debunks
Animosity by example junks
Partisanship and with compassion pours
Out his wisdom with loving-kindness
Bringing sunshine to unhappy people
Offering non-attachment and non-fear
With trust and confidence and mindfulness
Interpenetration is natural —
I hunger for peace — he serves as a spur.

For his *stupa* he requested
These words:

I am not in here
I am not out there either
I may be found in
your way of breathing
your way of walking.

I don't give myself to anything else
While slicing an orange and an apple
I allow my attention to be full
Of how the tips of my fingers hold the
Fruit with one of my hands — and of how the
Other guides the knife and keeps it stable —
The oranges are unpredictable —
Is it going to be a juicy or a
Dry orange? The knife goes through the apple
With just a tiny tug of resistance —
It's my habit to make quarter sections
And then to remove the inedible
Stem and the seeds to suit my preference
And there isn't any more to dwell on.

Anticipation
accompanies the
operation — will
the orange be sweet and
the apple honeyed?

This moment can be a seed of joy if
I follow what a crow is doing on
A branch and I notice it's bobbing on
One of the upper branches just as if
It's claiming a prominent perch as if
It's exerting a dominance upon
This little territory whereupon
It's bobbing and it's cawing in a riff
Of abrasive assaultive utterance
While I don't see any other bird or
Squirrels in the surrounding trees or on
The ground as it's casting a wary glance
Around — I don't know what is cawing for
And can't imagine what it's set upon.

Whatever the crow
was doing is beyond my
knowing as the world
is mysterious and now
the crow has moved somewhere else.

What can one say about the public schools
In Baltimore that fail to educate
Where even though the students graduate
They can't read and so they face a brutal
Existence guaranteed to have trouble
And yes I could have written boilerplate
Writing paragraphs that articulate
Who are the shamefully negligent fools
Responsible for the failing schools but
I don't have a clue about what to do
With the interlocked pattern of failure —
I think that fatherlessness is somewhat
To blame along with bureaucracy too
But there's so much heartache in Baltimore.

I only wrote the word
"Baltimore" once along
with Chicago and
New York as examples of
cities with gang violence.

In January in Baltimore there
Were 36 homicides and the
Police appear demoralized and the
Streets are controlled by the gangs who aren't scared
Of arrest because officials declared
That violations of law aren't worth the
Effort of prosecution prompting the
Casual sales of drugs in public squares
And that is just as well because the state's
Attorney is under indictment for
Financial shenanigans which is not
Surprising because we shouldn't fixate
On one lawyer — it's all happened before —
As public corruption is a blind spot.

Baltimore is in
Washington D.C.'s blind spot
even though it is
only 40 miles away
Baltimore doesn't make news.

The president's press secretary on
A Zoom meeting kibitzed about the news
Business being light-hearted and amused
That one provoking channel makes her yawn
Assuming these reporters are morons
Or are sleazy as they purposely skew
The facts by overemphasizing views
That are so foolishly dystopian —
They live in an alternate universe
She says defending her president and
Party denying the mayhem and fear
In big cities — she believes it's perverse
That correspondents have such freedom and
She thinks that this network is cavalier.

The video of
her Zoom comments was
broadcast by the
network that she dislikes —
she needs to be more careful.

Without a person looking into it
A mirror resembles an empty box
It becomes a curious paradox
There isn't an ounce of meaning to it
The open sky and the clouds don't need it
A mirror is also like a tinderbox
It depends upon a jack-in-the box
And needs an anxious person to use it
Without a conscious human being the
Mirror merely reflects and doesn't grow
Or influence the things about it but
Once it does reflect a person's face the
Mirror casts a spell and births an ego
Inside an image a person gets shut.

A mirror without
a face is like a box
without a lid.

There often wasn't very much to do
Standing in the outfield playing baseball
Just watching and waiting for a flyball
With teenage fantasies to follow through
With insecurity clouding my view
Playing my role and expecting fastballs
Doubting myself and anxious of curveballs
I had to be speedy to muddle through
Inning after inning I was waiting
I hungered for the chance to prove myself
But I was relieved when nothing happened
Being on edge and anticipating
I knew that a test would impose itself
Earning acceptance — that's what I wanted.

All the practice with
catching groundballs and flyballs
was part of growing
up and I'm remorseful of
the flying ball that jinxed me.

It's just a convention to play with rhymes
And I know the easily rhyming words
The sense of the poem can't be absurd
As logic should follow from line to line
I would like the meaning to be benign
It's propitious to write about birds
Inside this book flamingos are preferred
Their oddness and loveliness do combine
Usually I am not serious
It's nifty to confabulate rhythm
I'd like to end with a surprising joke
Being awkward is deleterious
Could you type by using only your thumbs?
My favorite plant is the artichoke.

The president is serious
Oh so sanctimonious
But he doesn't deign
To often explain
I think he is delirious.

Is there a more sublime image than a
Chubby boy playing a tuba puffing
His cheeks pursing his lips and vibrating
The air with a marvelous um-pa-pa
A low reverberating oom-ba-ba
A lovely metaphor symbolizing
A musical rendering of farting
And as a rascal I'd like to add a
Humble dollop by dropping an empty
Snail shell into the tuba picturing
The combination of curves within curves
A happy symmetry in sympathy
With a symphony of rhapsodizing
Frivolous phantasmagorical verve.

Do you think the
snail shell in the
lowermost curve
of the tuba
would rattle?

I close my eyes and listen intently
And absorb the sound inside the shell of
A conch a lovely epitome of
Nature's fantastic creativity
Frolicking with my receptivity
Rollicking with nonsensical thoughts of
An ear listening to the sound inside of
Another ear — is this a bumblebee?
The sighing and swelling of an ocean?
Or the sprinkling of rain upon a lake?
Is this the rhythm of my heart and blood?
The breaking of waves in lazy motion?
I may be giving myself a headache
With the commotion of a sprightly flood.

The absent conch
has left behind
a lovely pink ear
that I can hear.

How handy fingers are for typing these
Letters as the impulse of thought obtains
Expression tapping the keys to explain
This lovely quiet morning and to tease
Curiosity to see and to seize
Upon the barren branches that contain
A pink tinge of light that only remains
For a moment that diffuses and leaves
The trees in daylight — and how useful are
My hands that handle the panoply of
Forms of all the thousands of things I touch
Without really noticing that they are
Voluptuously tactile and I love
To caress the world — without thinking much.

My creased
fingers and palms
are a bridge to
phantasmagoria.

Every morning before the bathroom sink
I turn the faucet and the water runs
Scrubbing with a soapy liquid is fun
I splash my face and use the time to think
Suds get in my eyes and I have to blink
While shaving my face I do tend to hum
I scrape the razor and it does drag some
In the mirror I see my face is pink
My bathroom serves as a sanctuary
Inside the shower my thoughts are popping
Cascading water helps inspiration
I'm blissfully warm in February
Soap shampoo conditioner are flowing
In my head there's snappy fermentation.

Innocently bare
nakedly present
without defenses
I am who I am
and mostly happy.

Thirty-eight Years Ago . . .

I would leave home in the early evening
With no idea of where I would go
Whichever location I'd be solo
Constant loneliness was suffocating
The prospect of women was inviting
I was a dispirited Romeo
Whatever might happen I didn't know
The rush of my drinking was exciting
I hunted for fun with friendly strangers
And tried to forget my inhibitions
I had no clue of my perplexity
And rode a wave of possible danger
Big city avenues were a come-on
Wanting love is an addict's elegy.

Carousing on the
empty avenues of
big cities alone at
night looking for excitement
only led me to dead ends.

A hole in my soul had ahold of me
I was hurting but couldn't admit it
If you had asked I would have denied it
My own behavior was a mystery
I barely acknowledged my misery
I made a show of being a misfit
And pretended that I even liked it
I thought of myself as being gutsy
By getting used to feeling embarrassed
I didn't like cold sweats and hangovers
My head didn't clear until afternoon
My thinking capacity diminished
I prided myself on being clever
Others had problems — *but I was immune.*

My life narrowed to
a dark corridor
of closed doors but
I didn't notice.

At the detox center I say to the
Volunteers that I drink usually
On the weekends and occasionally
I do smoke a little weed during the
Week but only as a way to take the
Pressure off and it is true certainly
If you had my problems you'd drink too — *see?*
I am not alcoholic — don't like the
Word but maybe I am dependent on
Drugs and alcohol to some extent — *and*
They say that dependence is another
Word for alcoholism — whereupon
I surrender all my arguments and
The burden of shame lifts from my shoulders.

I realized that
I wasn't a bad person
but I *had* this thing
alcoholism — that went
a way toward understanding.

"*If you had my problems you would drink too*"
I meant those words and thirty days later
In a halfway house and feeling better
I saw those words — *just as I said them too* —
Which was a happy case of *deja vu*
Beside a pool table on a poster
While playing a game with two New Yorkers
Inside a house many addicts passed through
Sharing the mission of getting sober
We talked to each other — we all got jobs —
Youthful desperate — *they were just like me* —
There was our dignity to recover
We didn't fool ourselves — *we faced long odds* —
Getting drunk or drugged is very easy.

How could addicts so
youthful with so much
life to live heap so
much trouble upon
themselves as to be
hopeless?

Something's broken in an addict's thinking
Whatever normal is — *we are not that* —
And it's a predicament to get at
We don't notice that we're isolating
And we're experts at manipulating
Turning our families into doormats
Being dishonest we get skillful at
To our loved ones this is disheartening
It's not intentional but it happens
We push our loved ones to a breaking point
And then they have to turn their backs on us
Sometimes we enter a fatal tailspin
Every addiction reaches an endpoint
Would the world be better off without us?

Near the end the addict
is a pathetic
combination of
confusion self-pity
and resentment.

It's a big deal to get an addict to
A corner where he wants to stop and the
Decision has to come from within the
Addict — there is nothing at all to do
Except to allow the addiction to
Continue inevitably to the
Point where the addict recognizes a
Breaking point — it's a bad idea to
Exert control or force on him or her
Because the addict can't be outsmarted
Or separated from the drug or drink
But the agony of addiction serves
Even though it seems to be coldhearted —
Through pain — *to change the way the addict thinks.*

Only too much pain
will bring about
the necessary
change of
heart.

Both of them at the detox center were
Crafty — they took the opportunity —
They got me talking and listened to me
The night before was a confusing blur
A half-remembered shameful drunken slur
I drove drunk — the police arrested me —
The volunteers were kind and talked to me
They asked if I wanted something better
And sidestepped my pride and didn't fight it
Suggested that things were going to get worse
They calmly discussed alcoholism
I was conflicted and admitted it
But I wasn't evil — wasn't perverse —
My world disintegrated — I was *numb*.

Alcoholics
know what to say
and how to say
it to cornered
alcoholics.

I admitted I was alcoholic
And a weight was lifted from my shoulders
I didn't know — *but I turned the corner*
My denials and defenses were thick
Kindness and understanding did the trick
It was helpful that I was hung over
The volunteers were patient and clever
I freely accepted that I was sick
Only after I admitted defeat
Could I finally grasp my misery
I was stubbornly scrappy every day
My excuses were full of self-deceit
I felt the anger but not self-pity
I had earned *a sobriety birthday.*

After talking to
the volunteers I
went to a cot
and slept like a
newborn baby.

Who could love you after what you have done?
After the hell that you have put them through?
Really what do you expect them to do?
The betrayal of love can't be undone
Yours was a devilish game of hit-and-run
Your lying stealing absence were taboo
Do you imagine that they still love you?
Loving a desperado isn't fun
Your predicament can't be fixed with words
Your apologies aren't good enough now
For the moment you have to let them go
You remember the things that you ignored
You'd like to be better but don't know how
You'd rather be numb than to feel so low.

The easy escape
from the unbearable weight
of remorse and guilt
gives the urge to drink or drug
a most demonic allure.

The first few days and months are critical
You can live usefully — *you're not alone* —
There's a better way — *you have to be shown* —
It's true you are a genuine oddball
You can never safely drink alcohol
What you need today is a buffer zone
And you don't have to suffer on your own
For *now* your thoughts are unreliable
Nothing is more important than these days
Drinking again is the same as *dying*
You are not alone — *you have loving friends* —
We gather such strength in our repartee
It is necessary to *stop lying*
So be honest with us and don't pretend.

You will never find
people who understand you
better than we do
as we share your impulses
and together we are strong.

Nobody comes to recovery on
The wings of victory and it's a good
Thing too because without a defeat *would*
You think over your denials and could
You let go of what you depended on?
So much of what you believed is a con
You played the role of willing victimhood
The world was against you from where you stood
You couldn't find the place where you belonged
Painful thinking was the fuel for drinking
You see the world with a lopsided view
It doesn't matter if you're right or wrong
It is self-pity that you are fighting
Your *ragged* anger isn't helping you.

What underlies
the abandoned urge
to drink other than the
wish to escape the way you
think the world is?

You are odd — *but you're not one of a kind* —
You can find us inside every city
Off the Baltic Coral or Greenland seas
You can connect with us at any time
There are plenty of meetings now online
Please don't allow yourself to be lonely
Our banter makes for the best company
In our rooms we leave our troubles behind
Life gets difficult in isolation
Sorrow is magnified by solitude
The police will hunt you after midnight
Attitudes change with communication
I don't see the world the way that I did
I breathe freely and flourish in sunlight.

Sobriety turns
wretched experience
into useful and even
lighthearted
stories.

It's going to take some time to clear your head
Your body is polluted with toxins
You've gotten used to abnormal rhythms
As often as possible you've been wired
When coming down you are *so very tired*
Excitement brings fantastic illusions
Then they flip to horrific delusions
You've put effort into getting *wasted*
What will life be like without chemicals?
Thinking about the future causes dread
There are so many things you've avoided
You think that starting over is futile
It would be better to get high instead
You know that your thoughts are convoluted.

The idea of
facing existence without
the comforting shield
of intoxication is
almost paralyzing.

You have thought you may be cheating yourself
You do wonder if you are really good
You'd like to live decently if you could
And you've prided yourself on being tough
Of all this misery — *you've had enough* —
If you could live without the pain you would
If there were a better way then you should
But it's true that you barely trust yourself
Taking a drug or a drink is easy
Like lightning — *in an instant* — it's *over*
It's *so* familiar to have failed again
You do wonder if you're just *too* lazy
When the urge *bites* you are a pushover
There is a strange comfort inside the pain.

The morning after
with a splitting head and a
sweating body you
think there's no way you're going to
do it again — *but you do.*

The urge comes suddenly and you submit
Getting high amid a neon aura
Hunting for moments of euphoria
What is authentic? What is counterfeit?
An addict does become a hypocrite
With a drug-induced schizophrenia
With a despairing sense of inertia
But a part of you is longing to quit
You get to know the names of policemen
You do receive their hospitality
You make appointments to speak with judges
You ape the role of a comedian
You're missing the taste of reality
Your life has become a depressing trudge.

Everyone you know
drinks and drugs like you do —
you don't have a
problem — you just need to be
a little more careful.

An arrest an accident a divorce
Are activities to look forward to
You know catastrophe is overdue
The urge to drug is a devilish force
It overwhelms the anguish of remorse
The nagging guilt and shame are biting you
You don't have a hint about what to do
You're not improving *but are getting worse*
You are aware of being a time bomb
You finally admit that you are *done*
Just how you will live you don't have a clue
Reaching the end is called *hitting bottom*
This is not victory — *it is not fun* —
You are a regretful mess of a stew.

When I admitted —
I am an alcoholic
and a drug addict —
a weight was lifted from my
shoulders and I felt relief.

Each of us will take a turn in speaking
We go around the room telling stories
We will talk about what we did *with ease*
Don't be surprised if you hear us laughing
Your company today is inspiring
We know every detail of your *dis*ease
Have suffered *splendidly* for expertise
We know what it's like to be despairing
We each *hit bottom* to come in the door
From your perspective nothing is funny
We are cheerful and happy to meet you
Ours is a fellowship of simple rapport
We *were just like you* but now we are *free*
Our lives gain such *meaning* by helping you.

Your presence in the
circle — *so raw and exposed* —
reminds each of us
of the absolute anguish
of those first slippery days.

You are happy because you've let it go
You've admitted you can't live as you did
If you try you will probably be dead —
You thought you could manage — *you let it go* —
You thought you were special — *you let it go* —
You ignored your misery and your dread
You made a big fool of yourself instead
Those years of denial — *you've let them go* —
You didn't know how hard you were fighting
Until the very moment you gave up
And weight came off your shoulders — *you relaxed* —
There is no reason to keep on lying
For decades the pressure was building up
And then in an instant it all collapsed.

All those years
of misery
led to a moment
of release that changed
nothing but your attitude.

There are facts about *you* you may not know
You had very little power to choose
You had turned into a slave of the booze
When the urge came on you couldn't say no
Alcohol and drugs are devilish foes
If you think you control them *you're* confused
They determined you — you hadn't a clue
Your guardian angels were a no-show
There once was an alcoholic who drove
From Minnesota to Las Vegas and
Back in a blackout and he returned to
Precarious consciousness inside of
A hospital psych ward in St. Paul — and
The gas receipts explained where he'd been to.

There will come a time
and a place where no human
power can save you
from the urge to drink — only
a *Higher Power* does that.

You can choose your own idea of God
God is inside you — *you may not know it* —
God is present — *you may not believe it* —
You may think that God is wickedly flawed
Perhaps the churches are empty facades
And the preachers' sermons are counterfeit
You've fought like a devil not to submit
You're defiant of phony demagogues —
Can you see that defiance gets in the
Way of reliance and that you've put up
Barricades — and we are not asking you
To submit but to find an idea
Of a Higher Power that will show up
When no other human touch can save you?

Certainty is not
necessary — you
only need to
sincerely seek.

Those first few days and months are difficult
There are times of genuine happiness
When having friends is a new kind of bliss
But then your emotions are *virulent*
Your nagging impulses are dissonant
Fear and self-pity make for crankiness
Envy and resentment lead to nastiness
Stubbornness renders you ambivalent
For the first time you're feeling emotions
When over years addiction made you *numb*
You do encounter the fuel of your fire
Your mind simmers with painful explosions
You are deathly afraid of days to come
But you resolve not to remain a liar.

Newly sober
you are like a turtle
who has lost its shell
to find that its skin is
exquisitely sensitive.

There are no barriers into our groups
Happily we are not strangers to you
All these tribulations — *we've felt them too* —
We know the emotions that make you droop
We share experience that made you stoop
There are practices that will pull you through
We survive and prosper — *so you can too* —
Think of all the burdens that you will drop
We do suggest that you choose one of us
Together you will learn our principles
And disperse the terror of your secrets
And relearn the gift of innocent trust
You can regain your courteous scruples
And make propitious use of your wits.

Among us you will find
survivor's euphoria
rascality gratitude
uncommon honesty
and hilarious stories.

Hang on to the moment you surrendered
The turning point when you became *willing*
It was either that or keep on dying
At a lonely abyss your mind opened
And a glimmer of hope reawakened
Cosmic circumstances were aligning
And infinite forces were conspiring
Do you really comprehend what happened?
You didn't lose before an enemy
You finally quit a hopeless battle
And just stopped being stupidly stubborn
You gave yourself the gift of clemency
The lesson here is unforgettable
Upon this foundation new life is born.

Relaxation amid
difficult circumstances
is the most precious
gift.

You needn't define your Higher Power
But you should admit that *you are not it*
Whatever *it* is — *just stop fighting it* —
For years your Higher Power was liquor
You gave chemicals all of your power
You consecrated the drugs with your habits
You honored sacraments with your vomit
The taste of your life was toxic and sour
You need to believe in something to live
Some kind of succoring beneficence
Churches temples and synagogues could do
You need something worthy to stay alive
Gather the power of good common sense
Come to believe this power is *in* you.

If you have trouble
believing in a Higher
Power for now just
suppose it *might* exist and
that it *could* help you to live.

No one can transfer this power to you
You can only find it *within* yourself
Perhaps you'll see that it grows *of itself*
It can provide such confidence to you
You'll gain integrity and knowledge too
You don't need to solve problems by yourself
As so many troubles will solve themselves
You may find the answers will come to you
The trick is *reliance — not defiance —*
You'll want to turn your life over to *it*
This undefinable something guides you
It's much better than your self-reliance
So good intentions and behavior fit
You will find the cosmos supporting you.

Having good intentions
giving your best efforts
while turning over
results to a **Higher Power**
summon relaxation.

People will ask me after 38
Years why I keep going to my meetings
Won't I ever be congratulating
Myself on being good and living straight
After so many decades why fixate
On memories that should be receding
As I've earned my sanity by proving
Myself recovered sharing not a trait
Of those desperadoes? But they don't know
I could easily become an addict
Again as our years of experience
Show that none of us is safe — time winnows
Us — *it is impossible to predict
Who will fall* — sobriety is a dance.

Because the pattern
of addiction lives in me
I can't afford to
indulge the attitudes that
are tinder to the burning.

Besides I've gotten used to a level
Of friendship and communication that
Is rarely found outside of our groups that
Is premised on honesty and good will
That out of our suffering we distill
The commonsensical principles that
Will defuse an exasperation that
Tempts me to burn it all to hell until
Nothing but ashes remains — *so you see* —
The devil is still inside of me and
Although I appear to be sensible
I do like my tinge of rascality
That does balance my integrity and
Renders me especially lovable.

You could say that a
recovered alcoholic
and addict may be
many things but certainly
not a predictable bore.

Edward Scissorhands

In a movie Edward Scissorhands is
A sweet creation of an inventor
Who died leaving no one to look after
Edward who's abandoned and left on his
Own in a mansion on a hill which is
Sad as Edward couldn't be lonelier
Edward is pure and couldn't be nicer —
It is a predicament that Edward is
Not finished as his creator didn't
Have the time to make for Edward *proper*
Human hands so he languishes alone
In a spooky manor and he doesn't
Have the occasion to receive and share
Genuine love — *Edward needs to be shown*.

Instead of having
the *soft palms and fingertips*
we take for granted
Edward possesses wires
and the sharpest of steel blades.

Then a woman named Peg who's an Avon
Lady selling cosmetics is having
Difficulty because she's not making
Sales so she ascends the hill and comes upon
The dusty empty mansion whereupon
She sees Edward in the dark cowering
In a corner — *and Edward is trembling* —
Doesn't know what to do — being withdrawn
Within himself for so long and meeting
Peg so suddenly is confusing and
Peg is taken aback by his scissor-
Hands but Peg is kindly considering
His forlorn abandoned existence and
His oddly benevolent demeanor.

Peg Boggs decides to
take Edward from the mansion
down the hill in her
car to live with the Boggs
in their *domicile* in town.

Edward's scissors are *multitudinous*
The many blades on each of his hands makes
Adapting to life difficult — it takes
Thoughtful effort to button a shirt — *plus* —
He's never had a comb — his hair's a mess —
So it's not strange that he suffers outbreaks
Of anxiety with throbbing headaches
But Peg expresses a feminine fuss
She shows him the marvels of a mirror
She provides him a sense of normalcy
He compares himself with everyone else
With a shock he perceives that he is weird
He's made aware of his deformity
He knows that he looks like nobody else.

Edward has the most
difficulty balancing
successfully a
pea upon a blade of a
scissor while eating supper.

Peg has a teenage daughter who is Kim
Is Edward attracted to her? *Sort of*
Does Kim suppose that he is odd? *Kind of*
Kim has never seen a person like him
Dangling razor-sharp mechanical limbs
Days before he couldn't conceive of *love*
Edward doesn't know what he's dreaming of
A captivating hypnotizing *whim*
He notices a *pang* in his stomach
He hasn't a clue about what to do
These new sensations only confuse him
Overwhelming longing that makes him *ache*
It's an exhilarating rendezvous
Poor Edward can't stop thinking about *Kim*.

Kim has a boyfriend
named *Jim* who smirks and jokes
about Edward's plight
balancing and dropping peas
at the family supper.

In town the women are interested
About this mysterious character
They speculate why Peg would sequester
The waif within her home separated
Suspiciously perhaps to be confined
And selfishly enjoyed which is *bizarre*
So that the frustrated ladies *concur*
It's proper that Edward be presented
To society and celebrated
And thereupon the women converge at
Peg's front door and they insist that she host
A barbecue for him to be *revealed*
So that everyone could mingle and chat
Where they will bring salads — with which to *boast*.

Joyce Monroe
insistently feeds
spoonfuls of her
ambrosia salad to
a confused Edward.

Even with the self-inflicted scars on
His face Edward is a handsome young man
And innocent too as the women can
Tell — *what erotica to come upon* —
What curiosity that Edward spawns —
They've never seen such unusual hands
Which do so much to stimulate their glands
His complexion is intriguingly wan
Edward has skillfully trimmed the hedges
About the yard and shown himself to be
An expert sculptor creating perfect
Statues of the Boggs family with his
Blades — it's obvious he is a marquee
Artist — captivating in all respects.

The ladies of the town
line up to have Edward
cut their hair in the
most *exotic* styles.

In addition to cutting women's hair
Edward trims poodles and shih tzus also
Women implore him — he doesn't say no —
He is innocent — why *should* he beware?
Celebrity is a happy affair
While he is shy his reputation grows
He appears on a variety show
Edward's vulnerable and not aware
He is pushed to open a hair salon
He's brought to a bank to secure a loan
With no Social Security number
Without any credit to draw upon
His employment history is unknown
They do ask him to try again later.

Joyce Monroe
leads Edward to the
back room of a proffered
salon *where she disrobes*
and *Edward runs away*.

On returning home Kim and Jim were locked
Out of the house and Edward unlocked the
Door with a little blade which gave Jim a
Nefarious and *sneaky* scheme that shocked
Kim — who really dislikes the way Jim mocks
Edward — Jim pushed Edward to unlock a
Door inside his Dad's house that leads to a
Guarded chamber and so Jim *concocted*
A plan and *bullied* Kim and Edward to
Break into the room and to burglarize
Money while his Dad was on vacation —
For the caper they dressed in black to do
The deed while Kim was unhappy and seized
With doubt and *dreadful anticipations.*

Jim was outsmarted by
an alarm that summoned the
the Police — Jim and Kim
escaped — *but Edward was
arrested.*

Edward's hands do look like lethal weapons
Edward was lucky that he wasn't shot
The police were nervous when he was caught
Those first moments were critical seconds
They were poised to shoot a barrage of rounds
"*Drop your weapons*" they said but he could not
Poor Edward was twisted in mental knots
He did his best to follow directions
Then the neighborhood ladies intervened
They got the police to lower their guns
And Edward was cuffed and taken to jail
He stayed overnight and then he was freed
Because the judge believed he wouldn't run
Peg and her husband Bill put up the bail.

The judge treated him
with leniency because
a psychologist
deemed Edward to be without
knowledge of *proper morals*.

From the beginning Kim was standoffish
All she could see was that Edward was odd
Tongue-tied and awkward and horribly *clawed*
But she notices that Jim is selfish
He's greedy dishonest and devilish
She's disgusted with his phony façade
She thinks that Jim's love for her is a fraud
Edward's entrapment is not what she wished
Kim is embarrassed in Edward's presence
She feels so ashamed and also guilty
Edward's in trouble — *so what can she do?*
Edward embodies innocent patience
Why did Edward come? Why did he agree?
Edward said because she wanted him to.

Kim is the only
one who sees the injustice of
Edward's circumstance
from a comprehending and
an *adoring* point of view.

Peg's husband Bill has a talk with Edward
While the family is having supper
He asks Edward which he thinks is better
With found money — would he give it to friends?
Would he claim it as his own and pretend?
The police would take it — *if he prefers*
Which course of action is really proper?
Edward's confused — *he doesn't understand* —
Saying he'd give it to *his family*
Bill and Peg are *disappointed* with him
Going to the police was the answer
They correct Edward but do it *gently*
They're unhappy to see him sad and *grim*
Edward's inarticulate — *he stutters*.

They assume Edward
attempted burglary to
obtain the money
to open the hair salon —
they think he's ignorant.

The ladies in town are doubting Edward
*Joyce suggests that there's something wrong with him
And Joyce is afraid for Peg's daughter Kim*
Edward has earned a criminal record
His raunchy behavior can't be ignored
In spite of his talent he may be dim
Prospects for honest redemption are slim
Joyce admits that she's frightened of Edward
At the salon *Edward accosted her*
Edward attempted to remove her clothes
Thank goodness she *escaped* and wasn't *raped*
Edward isn't shy — *he's an imposter* —
What he's capable of *only God knows*
His genuine nature is taking shape.

Among themselves the
ladies agree that Peg and
Bill are blameless but
they decide not to go to
Peg's yearly Christmas party.

Edward is lonely and disconsolate
Jim is furious and has threatened him
Jim has warned him to stay away from Kim
It is hard for Edward to concentrate
Edward turns to sculpture to compensate
Carving a large ice angel pleases him
It is true the angel resembles Kim
Like snow the ice crystals accumulate
Edward is absorbed and lost in his work
He doesn't know that Kim is watching him
Kim is moved and dances within the snow
Kim is *enraptured* with Edward's artwork
Her attitude has changed — *now she loves him* —
She *does adore* him — *but he doesn't know.*

With a sweeping flick
of a blade Edward inflicts
an *inadvertent*
slice into Kim's upreaching
palm — *as Jim has slyly seen.*

Jim exclaimed "Get the hell out of here — *freak* —
You can't touch anything without destroying
It completely — and if you're not leaving
Now then I am going to *kill you — you geek*"
Peg came on the scene — got scared — and she s*hrieked*
She saw Edward frightened and Kim bleeding
She took Kim inside — Edward was fleeing —
Edward felt so very shameful and weak
He hated himself — *which made him angry* —
And Edward ran without a place to go
And punctured the tires of cars on the way
The neighbors saw him — *Edward was scary* —
They saw that Edward was a tornado
Of swirling knives — *and today was doomsday*.

On Christmas Eve
the night of Peg's party
the neighbors called the police
to hunt for Edward who had
become a *maniac*.

Peg is sorry thinking about Edward
She realized she hadn't thought it through
Of what bringing him home could *really* do
To themselves — to the town — and to Edward —
She is upset regretful — *and she's scared* —
So much happened that she'd like to undo
The whole society has come unglued
But at the moment just where is Edward?
Thankfully it's true — Kim's not deeply cut —
She is only scratched slightly — *where's Edward?* —
She and Bill decide to drive and find him
They need to act before someone gets hurt
Both Bill and Peg are nervous and afraid
Edward's not safe — *they need to protect him.*

Peg thinks that after
all maybe it's better that
Edward return to
the mansion on the hill so
things could return to normal.

Edward's anger dissipated quickly
He meandered in a circular way
There wasn't any place to run away
He kept within the shadows stealthily
He returned to the Boggs' home quietly
Edward calmly bore his *naiveté*
He encountered Kim inside the doorway
She welcomed him apologetically
And Kim wanted Edward to embrace her
And Edward wholeheartedly longed to
But Edward Scissorhands whispered "I can't"
He knew he couldn't without hurting her
Once again — *he didn't know what to do* —
He could only repeat himself — "*I can't.*"

Kim wasn't so
easily dissuaded
from her expression
of affection — she
embraced Edward.

Jim was driving and hunting for Edward
He was crazy and drinking heavily
He was furious and drove stupidly
Kim's brother Kevin visited a friend
It was late and he was walking homeward
Kevin was tired and walked unconsciously
Jim was drunk and swerving dangerously
Edward saw them both — *and so it happened* —
Edward rushed to the scene and then he lunged
He knocked Kevin safely out of the way
Jim barely missed them — *he screeched to a stop* —
Edward and Kevin became excited
And both of their arms were flailing away
The neighbors were watching and called the cops.

To the neighbors
it seemed that Edward
was attacking and
cutting Kevin
with whirling blades.

Edward Scissorhands is a poor fellow
He can't touch people as he would like to
And he's perplexed about what he *can do*
The scene on the street was a wild tableau
A swarming mob became a volcano
Jim jumped on Edward and a fight ensued
Edward defended himself — *his arms corkscrewed* —
Jim was sliced and slashed and so he bellowed
Peg and Bill arrived and rescued Kevin
People swarmed on Edward and they got cut
Edward got to his feet — *began to run* —
The empty mansion was his direction
Edward was appalled and knew in his gut
What had happened could never be undone.

A police cruiser
followed Edward
to the gates of
the mansion and
four shots were heard.

The boiling mob on the street followed on
Kim checked on Kevin and came along too
She was scared about what the mob would do
Housewives and husbands were running along
They were shouting howling coming on
Such a commotion on the avenue
Kim came to the gate and she ran on through
What happened to Edward — *where had he gone?*
"It's over it's over so please go home"
The policeman yelled — *and then he drove away* —
The crowd was angry and dissatisfied
They were enraged — *no one was going home* —
They were frustrated *crazed* and hunting *prey*
Edward's a monster and *must* be finished.

The iron gate to
the mansion on the
hill was down on the
ground and the road
wound upwards.

Kim came to the mansion and saw the grounds
There was a garden — and sculpted hedges —
And there were flowers along the edges
She entered the mansion and then she found
A broad stepped staircase and upward she bound
In the highest chamber — there Edward was —
She believed he was killed but *here* he was
She cried with relief — *wound her arms around
Him* — Edward was frightened — *out of his head* —
Only for moments the lovers embraced
She told him Kevin was really OK
She was so sorry — *she loved him* — she said
But just for mere seconds could she embrace
Him — on this *beastly cataclysmic* day.

Jim bolted in
the room holding
a gun — he aimed
and shot at Edward
but missed.

A part of the roof caved in upon Jim
He was startled and let go of the gun
Edward knelt down and he looked to be stunned
Jim seized a beam and savagely beat him
Jim was obsessed and forgot about Kim
He was determined — *had only begun* —
Kim would never forgive what he had done
She took an iron poker and hit him
Jim turned upon Kim and he knocked her down
Edward stood up and pressed blades to his chest
Edward pushed forward and the blades went through
Jim fell from a window — *dead on the ground* —
The mob was approaching — *Kim couldn't rest* —
She said *goodbye* — as she was *forced* to do.

Kim grabbed some scraps
of blades hung
on a rack — she
ran down the stairs
and out the door.

Then Kim confronted the mob at the door
She told them that Edward and Jim were dead
They battled and killed each other she said
No one in there is alive anymore
They could see for themselves — *just through the door* —
"You can see these blades for yourselves" she said
The crowd dispersed and went home instead
They thought they had got what they lusted for
Kim decided to go — *to leave Edward* —
She knew that he couldn't be safe in town —
Many years have passed — *Edward lives alone* —
Kim is full of remorse about Edward
He is protected and shouldn't come down
She's sorry he has to live on his own.

*Her eyes often
return to the
mansion on the
hill especially
on Christmas Eve.*

Kim is *certain*
she sees ice crystals floating
flowing from the
mansion — *perhaps Edward is
sculpting an angel of her.*

—*Tekkan*

www.ingramcontent.com/pod-product-compliance
Lightning Source LLC
Chambersburg PA
CBHW051551010526
44118CB00022B/2661